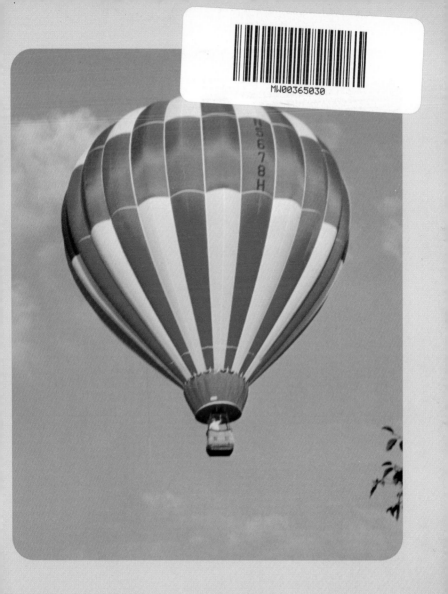

There are many ways
to go places.

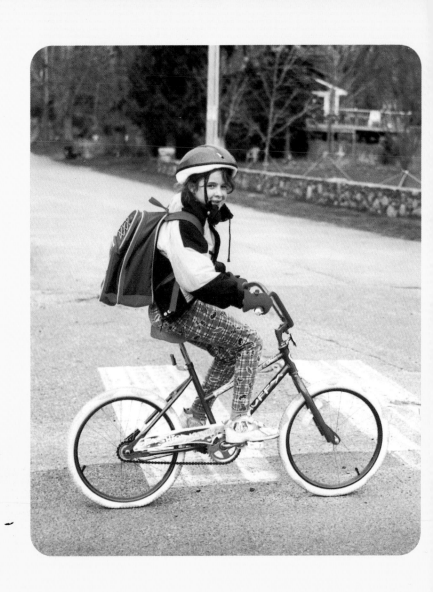

She rides a bike.

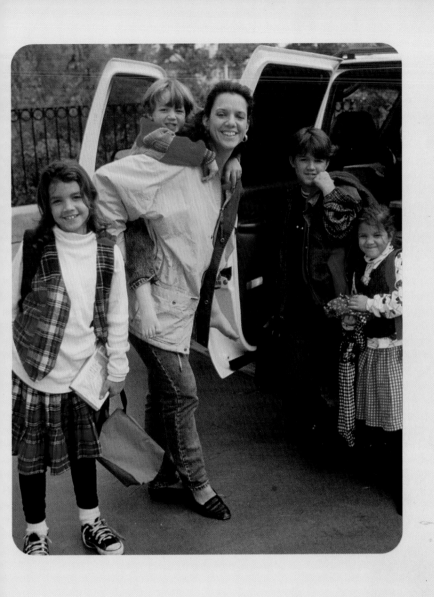

They ride in a car.

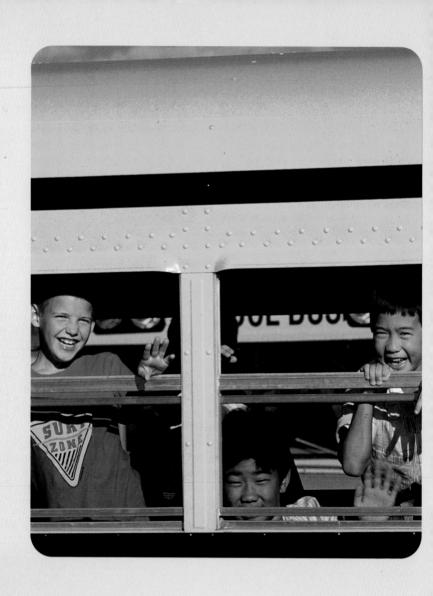

We ride in a bus.

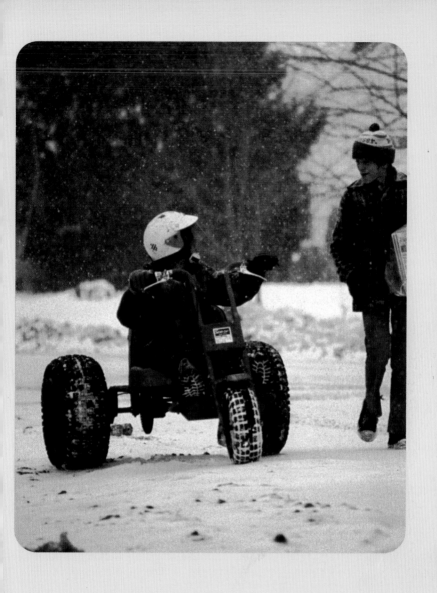

He rides a snow bike.

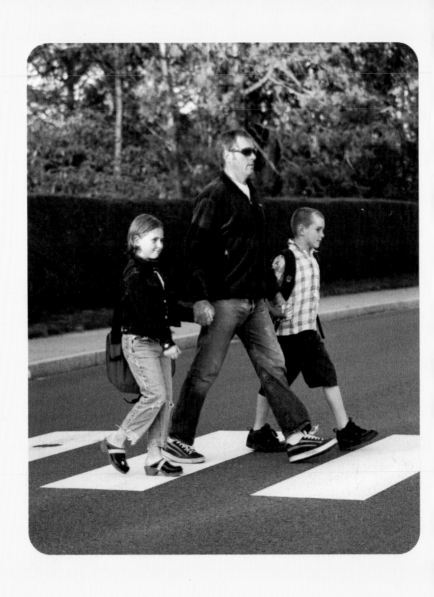

They walk.

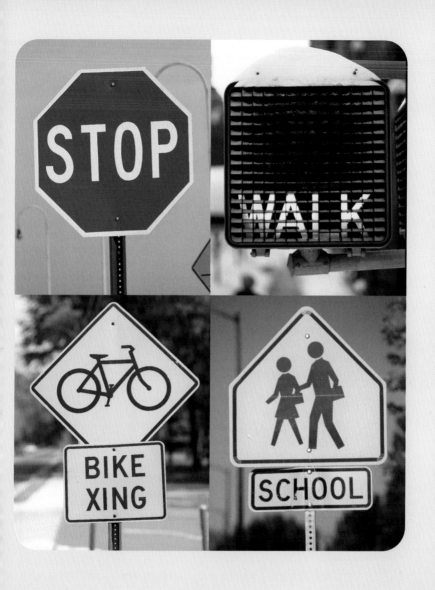

Signs help us to go places.

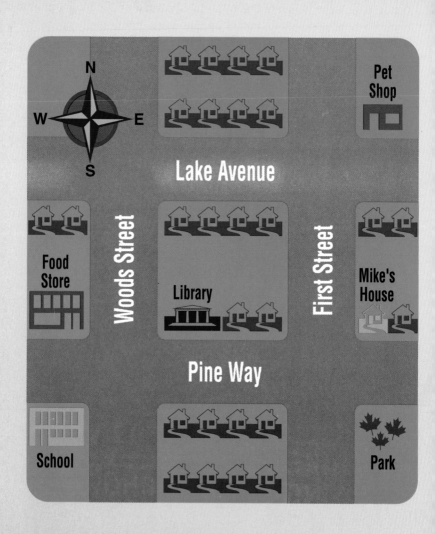

Maps help us, too.
Do you know how
they help?